T

R

D1347710

Kr

More great reads in the SHADES 2.0 series:

The REAL TEST

Jill Atkins

Ransom

SHADES 2.0
The Real Test
by Jill Atkins

Published by Ransom Publishing Ltd.
Radley House, 8 St. Cross Road, Winchester, Hampshire SO23 9HX, UK
www.ransom.co.uk

ISBN   978 178127 628 0
First published in 2014

CONTENTS

Ryan had a bounce in his step and a smug grin on his face as he made his way home.

It had been a cinch. No trouble! He didn't know what everyone always made such a fuss about. He gripped the sheet of paper firmly in his hand.

He was looking forward to flashing it in front of Mum. She'd said he wouldn't do it.

She'd have to eat her words.

Of course, he'd been nervous beforehand. He was human, after all.

But he'd made no mistakes, done everything the old buffer had told him, done it like a dream.

He was a natural. He couldn't wait to tell everyone.

'Hi, Ryan!'

Ryan froze mid-step when he heard the call from the other side of the road. He'd know that voice anywhere. It was Mollie.

He looked across the road, his heart on turbo-power. Wow! There she was, stunning as ever, even in that uniform. She must be on her way home from school on the other side of town.

'Did you pass?' Mollie called.

'Yeah!' he shouted, waving the evidence above his head. 'First time!'

Mollie dashed across the road. She reached up and gave him a hug.

His whole six-foot-two body turned to jelly. He felt his knees buckle and his head spin. Was it the rich brown of her eyes that did it to him? Or her elegant figure? Or that mass of black hair? Or was it the perfume?

She'd been going around with his mates for a couple of months and he'd fancied her from the start.

He'd never forget the day he spotted her down at the club, dancing in the middle of the crowd. There was no way he could have missed her. She was carried away by the beat, her body swaying with the music. Gorgeous.

It felt like he was struck by a flash of lightning. Sheer electricity!

He came back to the present. Mollie was

smiling up at him.

'Great!' she said. 'So when do we get to go out in your car, then?'

Ryan smiled back. He felt warm all over. First, he'd passed his driving test. Second, Mollie Andrews had given him a hug, and third, it seemed she'd just asked him out.

'My mum's car, you mean,' said Ryan, trying to look cool.

There was no point in pretending it was his car. Mollie must know he couldn't afford one of his own, even an old banger like Mum's. Not on the pittance he got for his Saturday job at the depot.

'Your mum's car then,' said Mollie as they began to walk along the road.

She doesn't seem to mind. Is it just me she wants?

'But it's as good as mine,' he lied. 'She'll let me use it any time I want. I only have to say the word.'

'Great!' Mollie said again.

'What are you doing tonight?' asked Ryan. 'We can go anywhere you like.'

If mum will let me.

When they got to his house, there were two people in the kitchen, his best mate Jordan and his younger brother, Kev.

'I passed!' Ryan announced, as he burst in at the back door with Mollie right behind him.

'You jammy devil!' laughed Kev. 'First time? You must have brown-nosed!'

Everyone laughed.

'No!' said Ryan. 'I was just brilliant. Perfect reverse round the corner. Perfect hill start. Perfect emergency stop. In fact, perfect driver!'

'And modest with it,' said Mollie.

'Seeing will be believing!' said Jordan. 'When do we get to witness your perfect driving?'

'We're all going out in his mum's car tonight,' said Mollie.

'You're on!' said Jordan.

'But … ' Ryan frowned.

He didn't want Jordan to come. He wanted it to be just him and Mollie. There he was, thinking Mollie wanted a date, but perhaps it was only the car she was interested in.

He looked at her and she smiled. He felt his heart miss a beat. Then he heard his brother laugh.

'You'll be lucky,' said Kev. 'I'll bet you a fiver Mum won't let you drive the car. You know what she's like.'

Ryan forced a smile. He wished Kev hadn't said that. Not in front of Jordan and

Mollie. He punched his brother's shoulder.

'Don't worry,' he said. 'She'll let me have the car all right and I'll be five quid up by tonight.'

But he wished he could be so sure.

TWO

Ryan was mad.

As soon as Mum had come in from work, he'd made her a cup of tea to get her in a good mood.

They went in the front room and sat down.

'You haven't asked me how my test went,' he said, as she sipped her tea.

'Oh, sorry. I forgot,' she said. 'I've been that busy at work. How did it go?'

'I passed!' he said, proudly showing her his Pass Certificate.

'Well done!' she said, but she didn't sound that excited.

Was now the right time to ask her? She was sitting with her head resting on the back of the chair and her eyes were closed. He took a deep breath and dived in.

'So I was wondering if I can have the car tonight?'

Her eyes opened, but no other muscle moved. Then she closed her eyes.

'No.'

She spoke so quietly he thought he'd imagined it, but she opened her eyes again and looked at him.

'No,' she repeated, with a shake of the head.

What a waste of effort getting her a cup of tea!

'Why not?' he shouted.

'I'm going round to Helen's tonight,' said Mum. 'I need the car myself.'

'Can't you go round there another night?'

'Do I have to spell it out? You can't have the car this evening.'

'But I've *got* to have it, Mum.'

'Got to? What do you mean, you've *got* to?'

'I've promised my mates.'

'Well, you'll have to un-promise them, won't you?'

'Mum!' Ryan was disgusted. 'How can you do this to me?'

He was sure she was making it up. She just didn't want him to have the car.

'I could drop you off at Helen's house. Then I could have the car.'

'And how do you expect me to get home?' she asked.

However much Ryan argued, she wouldn't change her mind.

In the end, he stormed out of the room, slammed the door and stomped up to his bedroom. It was just his luck to have such a mean, miserable mother.

A few moments later, his bedroom door flew open. Kev stood in the doorway, grinning.

Ryan was ready to throttle him. He knew what his rotten brother had come for.

'That'll be a fiver,' said Kev, holding out his hand.

Ryan delved in his pocket and slapped the note hard onto his brother's hand. He said nothing. He was seething too much.

'Easiest money I've ever earned,' laughed

Kev, as he backed hurriedly out of the room.

Ryan sat down on his bed and tried to think. How was he going to tell Jordan? He could make you a laughing stock in a second.

All because your stupid mum was so mean.

Even worse, how could he tell Mollie? It would ruin his chances. She wouldn't want to go out with a nerd who was under his mum's thumb.

He would have to ring them both and bluff his way through.

He decided to call Jordan first.

'Change of plan,' he began cheerfully. 'I'm not having the car after all tonight.'

'So Kev was right, was he?' laughed Jordan. 'Mummy won't let you have it!'

'It's not like that,' Ryan lied. 'I'm saving

the Big Night Out for the weekend. How about if we just meet down the club tonight?'

'If you like.'

Jordan didn't sound convinced, and Ryan was sure he heard a snigger down the phone. Would Jordan give him hell?

It wasn't quite so easy telling Mollie.

'Er … Mollie,' he muttered when she answered her phone.

'Oh, hi, Ryan.' Her voice was bright and cheerful. She sounded pleased it was him. He imagined her smile and his heart sank to his size twelve boots.

'It's like this …' he stuttered. 'Jordan and me thought … it would be real cool … if we all met down the club tonight instead.'

He'd been trying so hard to sound casual, but he knew he had made a right pig's ear of it.

'Oh.'

He tried to explain, but felt less and less convincing. 'We could do the car thing at the weekend.'

What must Mollie think of him?

'It doesn't matter,' she said, but her voice had lost its brightness.

He felt like killing his mum.

The evening was a total disaster. Jordan made sure everyone knew how pathetic he was.

But the worst of it was that Mollie didn't even turn up!

THREE

The rest of the week dragged on. Several times, Ryan psyched himself up to ask Mum, but each time he chickened out at the last minute.

So when Saturday arrived, he still hadn't asked her. And he hadn't seen Mollie. Was she avoiding him?

As he hurried home from work, he

decided he'd give the car a wash. Make it look like less of a wreck. Anything to impress.

But it wasn't there.

He dashed into the house and burst into the kitchen.

'Where is it?' he yelled, red-faced and angry.

'Where's what?' Mum asked, stepping back from him as he towered above her.

'The car, of course! What have you done with it?'

'What do you mean, *what have I done with it?*' His mum's eyes were flashing with annoyance.

'I wish you wouldn't repeat everything I say,' yelled Ryan. 'The car isn't outside. So where is it?'

'It's in for its MOT,' said Mum, folding her arms. 'It went in yesterday and failed.

We have to wait till Monday for the parts!'

'I don't believe it,' he shouted. He thought his head was going to explode. 'You've done this on purpose. You must have known I needed the car this weekend.'

'You didn't say.'

'But why did you have to take it in *this* weekend?' he shouted, glaring down at her.

'Because the MOT ran out, of course,' she said, glaring back. Grow up, will you. Stop acting like a spoilt little brat!'

That really made him wild.

'So what am I going to tell everyone?'

'The truth,' said Mum, turning away.

'This is the second time I've let them down. They'll never let me forget it.'

'Don't be so pathetic,' said Mum. 'Calm down before you burst a blood vessel.'

Ryan seethed. He paced backwards and forwards across the kitchen.

The truth? They'd laugh at him. They'd think it was just a feeble excuse, like he was nervous of driving the car. He would have to pretend he was ill.

He practised speaking in a croaky voice, then got on the phone to Jordan again.

'You don't want to come near me,' he croaked. 'I think I've got a deadly dose of 'flu.'

Jordan grunted. 'See yer, then,' he said.

It was almost impossible to make himself dial Mollie's number. He hadn't spoken to her since he'd let her down on the day of his test.

In the end, he forced his shaky fingers to press the numbers.

'I'm sorry,' he croaked after he had explained his illness. 'I know it's the second time I've let you down. I promise there won't be a third.'

Mollie sounded sympathetic.

'Hope you feel better soon,' she said.

Ryan spent a very boring evening watching quiz shows on TV. He kept wondering what his mates were doing. What did Mollie think of him? Who was chatting her up?

What a way to spend your Saturday night!

All the following week, after Mum got the car back, she made excuse after excuse.

First, Gran was ill and Mum had to race round and care for her.

Then the cat had to go for her injections at the vet's five miles away.

Next, Mum's tooth fell out and she had to go to the dentist.

Then she had to go to the launderette.

Excuse after excuse after excuse!

By the following Saturday morning, Ryan

knew her game.

He was utterly sick of lying and making excuses to his friends. And he was tired of waiting.

He felt frustrated. He still hadn't driven the car a single metre since he'd passed his test.

He made up his mind. He would have it out with Mum.

FOUR

Ryan thought about it all day at work, so when he arrived home he was ready.

He rushed straight to the kitchen, where his mum was cooking.

'I know your game,' he said quietly, trying to keep calm.

'Game?' said Mum. 'What game?'

'Oh, come on,' said Ryan, feeling his

anger rising. 'Don't play the innocent one. You've spent the last week and a half making sure I can't have the car.'

Mum turned from the cooker and faced him.

'What do you mean?'

'You've thought up every excuse under the sun. Be honest. You don't want me to drive the car at all, do you?'

'Well … I suppose you're right … '

'I knew it!' he shouted. 'I've been made to look a complete loser, thanks to you.'

'Don't be silly, Ryan!'

'I'm not. I'm dead serious. You've no idea what grief you've caused me.'

He put his hands on his hips and glared at her.

'So I want to know why.'

'Isn't it obvious?'

'No!'

Mum frowned.

'Old as it is, I want my car kept the way it is – in one piece!'

'It'll be all right. I *have* passed my test!'

'Yes, I know, but I don't want you going and getting yourself killed.'

'Oh, for God's sake!'

Ryan felt he was going to explode. She always had the knack of turning everything round. It was emotional blackmail.

'You're only just beginning to learn to drive,' said Mum. 'The real test is when you get out there behind the wheel.'

'So how am I supposed to get out there behind the wheel if you won't let me?'

'I could take you out for some practice … '

'That's ridiculous! A test is a test. And I passed.'

'But … I … '

Ryan forced himself to calm down. It

sounded like his mum was running out of arguments. If he played it cool, with a bit of luck, maybe she'd see sense.

'I won't drink, if that's what you're worried about,' he said more quietly.

'You'll drive too fast. Death on the roads, that's what young drivers are. Sorry, Ryan, but you're *not* having the car.'

And that was the end of it. So much for his hopes!

He stormed out, slammed the back door and marched blindly down the alley and into the street. He sat on the front wall, staring at the car – the car he wasn't allowed to drive.

How could she refuse to let him go out in it? There was no way he was going to look small in front of Jordan any longer.

And what about Mollie? If he couldn't take her out in the car, he might not get another chance with her.

'I'll show Mum,' he muttered.

He heard the phone ringing inside the house. The front door opened and Kev stuck his head out.

'It's for you!' he yelled.

Ryan dashed indoors, hoping it would be Mollie. It was Jordan.

'Where are we going tonight?' he asked.

Ryan had to think quickly. He couldn't tell Jordan the truth.

'Got any ideas?' he asked.

'How about a pizza?' said Jordan. 'Then we could see a movie. There's a good one on at the multiplex.'

'All right, I'll ring Mollie.'

'Get her to bring her friend, Shaz, will you?' said Jordan. 'I fancy her.'

Ten minutes later, Ryan stood looking at

himself in the mirror in his room. Mollie had said she could come and she'd bring Shaz. He'd promised to pick them up at 7.30.

'You've done it now,' he said to his reflection.

He'd have to take the car.

FIVE

As Ryan got ready, he started feeling guilty. It wasn't going to be as easy as he thought. His brain was doing overtime trying to psyche himself up to do it.

He went through the arguments in his mind.

'*How can I just breeze down to the kitchen and whip the keys?*'

'Cinch! You're only borrowing the car for a while. Mum won't mind really. She just fusses, that's all.'

'But suppose she needs the car this evening?'

'She can't have it all her way! It's about time you had a turn.'

'But what will she do when she finds out?'

'She'll just moan at you! And you can take that! You're used to it!'

He knew he shouldn't be taking Mum's keys, but he was desperate. He couldn't let the others down.

Anyway, this was his first date with Mollie.

He couldn't miss that. Not again.

He heard Kev go out about 7 o'clock. At 7.15, he opened his bedroom door and listened. The TV was on in the front room. Mum must be in there.

He crept downstairs and peered through a crack in the hinge. She was sitting with her back to the door.

He heard her laugh.

Good! She was enjoying some rubbishy programme. At least he wouldn't have to sit and watch it, like last weekend.

Tiptoeing to the kitchen, he took the keys off the hook and quietly slipped out.

He was glad it was dark. Nobody saw him unlock the car door and climb in. He buckled up, turned the key in the ignition and heaved a sigh of relief as the engine coughed into life first time.

Quickly, he put it in gear and headed off down the road.

He'd driven it loads of times with his mum when he was learning to drive, but now it felt like stealing, stealing from her.

If she had let you borrow it you wouldn't

need to be doing this.

He looked in the rear-view mirror. Mum hadn't rushed into the street. She was glued to the TV and hadn't noticed he had gone. But there would be trouble …

'Snap out of it!' he said to himself, as he drove round the corner. 'Stop being such a wimpy kid! Enjoy yourself.'

It was great being alone in the car, after having someone else sitting beside you telling you what to do. He was relieved too that he hadn't forgotten how to drive.

Jordan was waiting for him outside his house.

'So your mum let you have the car, then?' he said, as he got in and fixed his seat belt.

'Something like that,' said Ryan, grinning.

He didn't feel good about it, but wasn't going to let on to Jordan. He put his guilt to the back of his mind. He'd got one up on Jordan. Jordan hadn't passed his test.

Ryan felt excited about picking up Mollie. It was a pity the others would be there, too, but he'd have to put up with that. It was going to be a great night.

The girls were ready when Ryan and Jordan knocked on Mollie's door.

'Hi,' Ryan said to Mollie, suddenly feeling shy.

'Hi.'

'Only two weeks late!' said Shaz sarcastically.

Ryan tried to ignore her, but she bugged him. He turned his back on her and smiled at Mollie. He smelled her perfume and looked into those brown eyes. His knees melted like chocolate.

'I've been looking forward to this!' Mollie said.

'So have I!'

He couldn't think of anything else to say. She looked great in her skinny jeans and black top. She took his breath away.

Mollie smiled at him, then she ran to the car and jumped in the back with Shaz.

'All right, Sebastian Vettel,' laughed Shaz. 'Let's see how fast you can go.'

Ryan looked at her in the mirror and gave her a filthy look.

He didn't like the way she'd said that. She'd always been a loud-mouth, but she didn't have to make jokes about his driving.

'OK, then,' he said. 'Here we go!'

SIX

Ryan felt like he had been driving all his life. He could sense the others were impressed. Even Shaz!

He felt a warm glow of pride as he skilfully parked the car in the High Street.

So far so good!

In the pizza place, he sat next to Mollie, aware of her body close to his.

After a while, she slid up even nearer to him and smiled. Things were looking good.

'You're a brilliant driver,' she whispered.

'Thanks.'

He ordered his pizza in a dream and found himself eating it like a zombie.

He was so smitten with Mollie he almost forgot they were going to the cinema afterwards.

'All right?' he murmured when he'd finished.

'Yeah!'

She looked up shyly from under those thick, long lashes. It seemed she was as smitten as he was. Ryan's heart raced.

Suddenly, Shaz broke the spell.

'Come on, guys!' she laughed loudly. 'Anyone can see you're dying to get at each other. Just wait until we're in the cinema, will you?'

Jordan sniggered. 'Yeah, we'll miss the start of the movie if you two don't put each other down.'

'I haven't touched her!' said Ryan.

'Yet!' laughed Shaz.

Ryan glanced at Mollie. Her face was scarlet. He guessed his was, too.

When they had paid, Mollie ran out to the car with Shaz.

Ryan could hear them giggling. He didn't like Shaz. He wished he could have come alone with Mollie.

As he started the car again, he suddenly wondered if Mum had realised it was missing. He hoped she'd be enjoying the TV too much to notice.

What would she do? Call the police? Say it had been stolen?

She'd guess who had taken it. She'd be very angry. He'd have to face up to her when he got home. No problem. He could handle Mum.

Or could he? He'd be able to sneak back in later, when she was in bed, and she wouldn't ever know.

Anyway, he wouldn't let it spoil his evening, especially now things were going so well with Mollie.

The multiplex was five miles away in the next town. Ryan drove the car out of town and turned along the country road.

With each mile he grew more confident. Mum didn't know what she was talking about. Fancy saying you only started learning to drive after you'd passed your test.

The road was dark and winding, but Ryan didn't mind. He knew it like the back of his hand.

He could hear Mollie and Shaz whispering and giggling in the back. He smiled at Mollie in the mirror, as another car's lights lit up their faces. She smiled back, then looked away.

Yes! He was onto a winner!

SEVEN

'Doesn't this old car go any faster?' Jordan asked. 'My dad's does a hundred easily.'

'So does this,' Ryan lied. 'On the motorway.'

'What's it doing now?' laughed Shaz. 'Twenty?'

Jordan leaned over and looked at the speedo.

'Only forty,' he said.

'*Only forty?*' Shaz squawked, sounding like a parrot. Ryan wanted to wring her neck!

'Ryan,' Jordan teased. 'You're just like my great grandad. He only does forty max. He reckons that's a *nice* speed! You're a danger on the road when you drive too slowly, you know that?'

Ryan nodded, keeping his eyes on the road ahead. His nan was the same.

'But it's dark,' he said. 'And there are loads of bends.'

Shaz squealed with laughter.

'Ooooo, d'you hear that, Jordan? The boy's chicken!'

She was getting right up his nose.

'Shaz … ' whispered Mollie.

'You don't want Mollie to think you're a loser, do you?' smirked Jordan.

Ryan could have handled it if they had left Mollie out of it. But he couldn't let her think he was a loser, as Jordan put it.

So much for best mates. At this moment, he hated Jordan almost as much as he hated Shaz.

'Of course I can drive faster,' he snapped.

'Prove it!' shouted Shaz, right in his ear.

'Shut up, Shaz,' whispered Mollie.

But Shaz ignored her.

'If you dare!' she shouted.

That did it! Ryan suddenly felt himself snap. He gripped the wheel fiercely.

'Right!' he said, pushing his foot hard against the pedal. 'How do you like this?'

The car surged forward. Jordan leaned over to watch the speedo as the needle crept slowly upwards.

'Forty-five … ' he said.

'Only forty-five?' squawked Shaz.

'Fifty ... is that *it?*' jeered Jordan.

Ryan could feel his heart beating very fast. He was angry and a bit scared, but he also knew he was excited.

It was a great feeling, taking the bends like he was on a Grand Prix track. He'd been a fan of Sebastian Vettel for ages.

He hoped Mollie was still impressed by his driving. He looked in the rear-view mirror, but he couldn't see her face. She had the window open and the wind was blowing through her hair.

'Fifty-five ... ' said Jordan.

'Only fifty-five?' shrieked Shaz.

Ryan's foot pushed harder against the pedal. He would show them who was chicken!

'Sixty ... ' shouted Jordan. 'Go, man, go!'

Suddenly, Ryan saw a sharp bend ahead. He knew he was going too fast.

He jammed his foot on the brake, but the car didn't seem to want to slow down.

His knuckles shone white on the steering wheel, as the blinding lights of another car swung round the bend from the other direction.

He half closed his eyes, trying to see.

There was a squeal of tyres and the loud blast of a horn.

He heard Mollie scream as their car skidded sideways and hit the bank at the edge of the road.

'Hell!' Jordan yelled. 'Watch what you're doing!'

Ryan had no time to think. Things were happening too fast.

And there was nothing he could do!

Crash!

The other car hit them side on.

Smash!

Ryan clung onto the wheel as the car began to roll.

The girls' screaming and the car's rolling seemed to go on forever.

EIGHT

Suddenly, the car smacked up against a tree, still at last.

The screaming had stopped. There was silence, apart from the hissing of the car engine in the darkness.

Ryan shook himself and tried to clear the dizziness from his head.

He felt such pain in his legs it took his

breath away. He bit his lip, but that didn't help. He tried to move his legs, but he couldn't get either of them free. They were trapped.

He began to panic. What if there was a fire? They would burn to death.

He struggled and tried again to move his legs, but they wouldn't budge. And the steering wheel was right against his chest. How was he going to get out?

At that moment, it hit him.

He'd done exactly what his mum said he would do. He'd driven too fast.

'Death on the road,' she'd called it. He wished *he* was dead!

Death on the road? Mollie? Jordan? Shaz? Were they hurt? Just stunned like he was? Or were they dead?

He reached up and switched on the car's internal light.

Jordan was lying forward with his head on the dashboard. There was blood oozing from a deep gash down the side of his face. His eyes were closed. He looked terrible.

Why did Mum have such an ancient car? A more modern one would have had decent air bags.

'Jordan?'

There was no answer.

'Mollie? Shaz?'

Not a sound.

He looked in the mirror.

No sign of the girls.

Moving very slowly, he managed to twist slightly in his seat and look over his shoulder.

His head spun. There was blood everywhere, amongst a mass of arms and legs and bodies.

But no sound. Silent as the grave.

What have I done?

He put his hands over his eyes, trying to blank out what he had just seen.

Why did I have to be so stupid?

There was a sound outside the car.

He took his hands from his face and blinked as torchlight blinded him.

The light gave him a flashback to that other car coming round the bend, the squealing tyres, the horn, the screaming, the crash as the car hit them then, worst of all, the car rolling and the thud as they hit the tree.

'Are you all right?'

Ryan heard a man's voice.

He felt too ill to answer. His legs were giving him hell. He watched the torch beam flash around inside the car.

'Oh my God!' said a woman. 'I hope the ambulance gets here in time!'

'Maybe it's too late already,' said the

man. 'There's not much sign of life in there.'

There was a groan. It made Ryan jump. It was Jordan. His eyes were open, but he hadn't moved. He groaned again.

'You OK?' Ryan whispered.

'I'll live,' groaned Jordan, his hand coming up to his head. 'What about the girls?'

'I don't know,' said Ryan.

He hated himself. What if he'd killed them? Why had he let Jordan and Shaz bug him? He should have just told them to shut it and driven in his own way.

Then he heard the siren and saw the flashing blue lights.

'The ambulance,' he said, but Jordan didn't answer.

And there was still no sound or movement from the back of the car.

He was finding it difficult to stay awake. The pain was too bad.

He couldn't stand it much longer. He was aware of people and voices and noise and more bright lights ... and Jordan groaning ... and the pain in his legs ... and the silence from the back of the car!

Then everything went black.

NINE

Ryan opened his eyes.

He was lying flat on his back, looking up at a white ceiling, with brightly coloured curtains all around him.

He couldn't make out where he was. Then he realised. In a hospital.

But why?

He knew what had woken him up.

Pain! His legs were killing him. He looked towards the bottom of the bed and saw a large raised dome over them.

Then he remembered. The crash! Being trapped in the car.

And the others. What had happened to them?

He tried to sit up, but fell back with a groan. A nurse pushed the curtain aside and hurried towards him.

'So you're awake at last,' the nurse said. 'I'm Martin, by the way. Righto, Ryan. Time to take your blood pressure ... let me put this cuff on your arm.'

He wrapped the long cloth around Ryan's arm and checked the machine that bleeped beside the bed.

'Good, that's fine.'

He smiled. 'You were in the operating theatre quite a while.' He pointed at the dome. 'Both legs badly broken – in plaster under there.'

Ryan nodded. He had guessed they must be.

'How are you feeling?'

Ryan looked up at him and shrugged his shoulders.

'Where are the others?'

Martin didn't answer. He undid the blood pressure cuff then looked across the bed and nodded.

Ryan hadn't noticed Mum sitting there. He turned his head away.

He couldn't face her. She must be angry, and that was putting it mildly, but he didn't want to hear what she was going to say. He didn't need telling he was an idiot. Or a murderer! His eyes filled with tears.

'Ryan.'

Mum didn't sound angry. Just quiet and

calm … and sad.

She touched his arm.

He sniffed. 'I'm sorry.'

'I know,' said Mum.

That was all. She didn't say, 'I told you so,' or nag or shout. That made him feel worse. Even more guilty.

'The others?' he whispered, turning to her. Her face was red and blotchy as if she'd been crying. 'How bad?'

'Jordan's all right. Just cuts and bruises and a broken collar bone. They kept him in here overnight. He'll be allowed home this morning.'

This morning? How long had he been out cold? It must have been some hours.

'The girls?' he whispered. 'The people in the other car? Mollie?'

Mum said nothing. Just bit her lip and shook her head.

Death on the roads.

'Dead?'

He couldn't bear it! He *was* a murderer! He *had* killed them, just because he wanted to impress Mollie. He had been so brainless.

He turned away again, unable to stop the tears.

'Not dead,' he heard Martin saying. 'But they're all injured. The people from the other car are out of danger. So is the girl called Sharon. But Mollie … is she your girlfriend? She's still unconscious.'

He'd never forgive himself for this. Never!

He wiped his eyes with the back of his hand as Jordan came through a gap in the curtains. He was limping. He had a wide bandage round his head and his arm was held tightly in a sling.

'My fault,' he said to Ryan.

What was Jordan saying?

'*Your* fault?' said Mum. 'You weren't driving the car, were you?'

'No, but me and Shaz bugged Ryan something rotten,' said Jordan. 'Told him he was a loser. Made him go faster. We wouldn't have crashed if we hadn't done that. I'm sorry.'

Mum frowned, but she didn't speak.

'My dad's here,' said Jordan. 'He's come to take me home. See yer.'

'Yeah. See yer.' Ryan raised his hand.

When Jordan had gone he asked, 'Where's Mollie?'

'Just along the corridor,' said Martin.

'I want to see her,' said Ryan.

'I'm not sure that's a good idea,' said Mum, looking up at Martin.

Ryan tried to sit up again, but the pain in his legs made him flop back down.

'*Please*,' Ryan pleaded.

Martin shrugged. 'I suppose it'll be all right,' he said. 'Just for a moment.'

'But I can't move.'

'No such word as *can't*. Come on.'

'I'll go and get a coffee,' said Mum. 'I'll be back in a tick.'

'OK, Mum.'

Ryan lay back as Martin wheeled the bed out of the ward. Every jolt sent the pain shooting up his legs, but he clamped his teeth tight.

Stopping by a door and pushing it open, Martin wheeled Ryan into the doorway.

Mollie was lying on a bed, covered by a sheet. There were tubes and wires sticking out everywhere. Machines bleeped, screens showed zigzag lines. A large bandage covered Mollie's head.

A man was sitting beside the bed. It must

be her dad. He glared at Ryan. If looks could kill, Ryan knew he would be stone dead.

He wished he was.

But as Martin began to wheel his bed away, Ryan saw a movement.

'Wait!' he said. 'She moved.'

Mollie's eyelids fluttered and slowly, her eyes opened. Her dad jumped to his feet and leaned over her.

She smiled up at him.

'Dad,' she whispered.

'Thank God!' said her dad.

Ryan understood exactly what he meant. He squeezed his eyes tight shut and crossed his fingers, like he used to do when he was a kid.

Please let her be all right.

He knew he'd have to face up to what he'd done when he came out of hospital,

but it would be a lot easier if he knew
Mollie was going to get better.

He sighed as Martin took him back to his
ward.

He felt heavy and tired.

Then, as he began to drift off to sleep, in
his head he seemed to hear his mum's
words ...

'*The real test ...* '